THE CREE EXPLAINED

FOR CHILDREN

CTS Children's Books

CONTENTS

Text by Elena Pascoletti

Illustrations by Tommaso D'Incalci and Roberta Leonetti

Translated by Pierpaolo Finaldi

The Apostles' Creed

From the very first days of the Church, Christians found short and simple ways to express and to pass on what they believed. These were based on the Bible and on what was taught by the Apostles.

With the **Apostles' Creed** we can say out loud what our faith is all about, the faith into which we were baptised. Because we all believe the same thing, we can call all other Catholics our brothers and sisters.

I believe in God, the Father almighty
Creator of heaven and earth,
and in Jesus Christ, his only Son, our Lord,
who was conceived by the Holy Spirit,
born of the Virgin Mary,
suffered under Pontius Pilate,
was crucified, died and was buried;
he descended into hell;
on the third day he rose again from the dead;
he ascended into heaven,
and is seated at the right hand of God the Father almighty;
from there he will come to judge the living and the dead.
I believe in the Holy Spirit,
the holy catholic Church,
the communion of saints,
the forgiveness of sins,
the resurrection of the body,
and life everlasting. Amen.

I believe in God, the Father almighty Creator of heaven and earth

THE FATHER WHO GIVES LIFE

Before anything else existed, God existed!

It's difficult to imagine, but our God, who is the Lord of life, has always existed from all eternity!

He created time itself and all things visible and invisible because **he is the only Creator**. God made the sky, the sun, the moon and the stars to give light to the world, to divide the day from the night, and to mark the passing of the seasons. He wanted the earth and the sky and the sea to be full of every different type of animal.

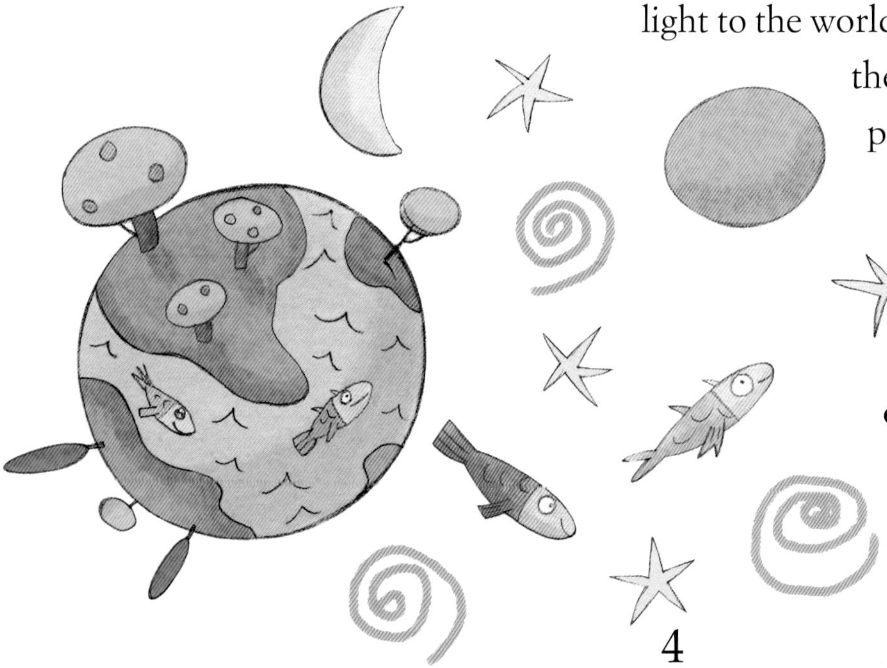

Finally he created man and woman in his image and likeness. He made them intelligent and free and able to love and to know God. God entrusted all of creation to them so that they could be responsible for looking after it with love and respect.

God created the universe to show us how much he loves us. In every creature we can see his goodness and his fatherly love. God is our Father! He takes care of every one of his creatures from the smallest to the greatest. For him we are small but precious, and he holds us in the palm of his hand.

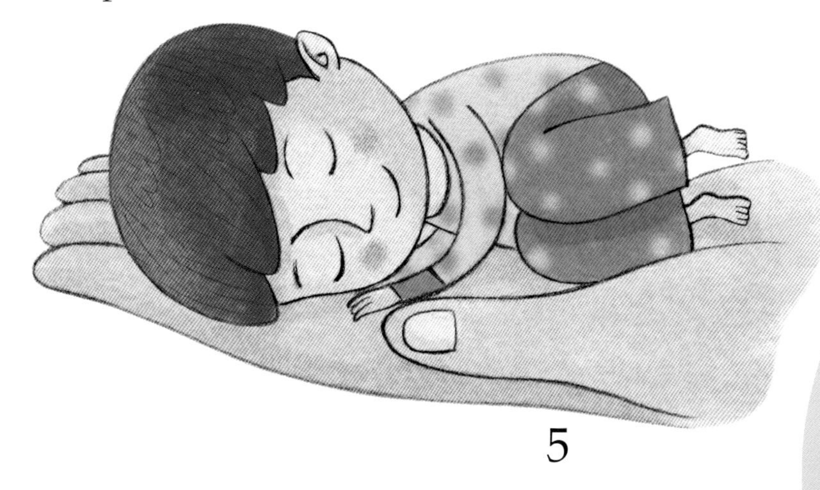

How many are your works, O Lord!
In wisdom you have made them all.
The earth is full of your riches.
Psalm 104:24

I believe in Jesus Christ, his only Son our Lord

THE SON WHO SAVES US

God promised his people that he would rescue them from slavery to sin. So he sent us his beloved son Jesus. His name means 'God saves'. He came into the world to tell everyone about the love of God. Jesus and God his Father are very close. Jesus said: "whoever has seen me has seen the Father". (Jn 14:9)

One day, Jesus went down to the river Jordan to be baptised by John. As soon as John had baptised him, an amazing thing happened. The heavens opened and the Holy Spirit came down on Jesus in the shape of a dove. God's voice could be heard from heaven saying: "This is my son, the beloved, and I am pleased with him". (Mk 1:11)

From that moment, God consecrated Jesus with the Holy Spirit. He said to everyone that Jesus was the Messiah for whom all the people of Israel had been waiting. The word Messiah means 'consecrated' or 'anointed'. In the Bible, people who had an important job to do for God were anointed with oil, especially the priests, the prophets and the kings.

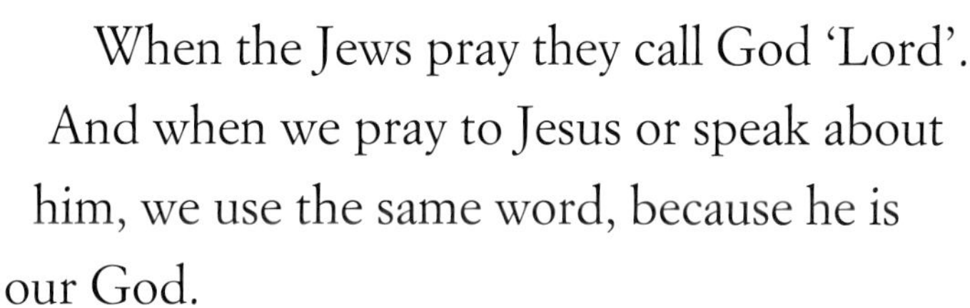

When the Jews pray they call God 'Lord'. And when we pray to Jesus or speak about him, we use the same word, because he is our God.

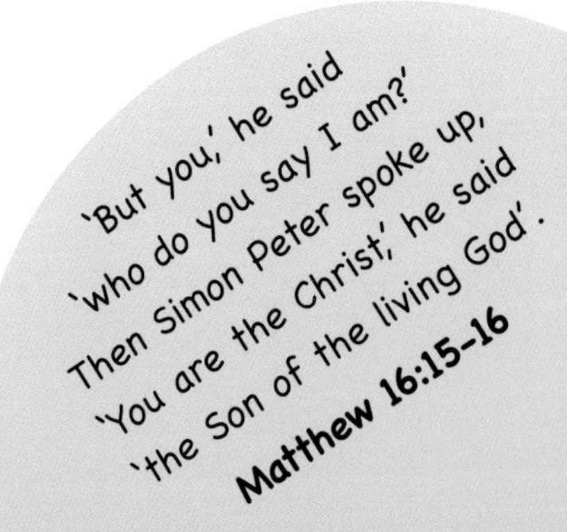

Jesus was conceived by the Holy Spirit and born of the Virgin Mary

THE SON OF GOD BECAME MAN

When God decided that the time was right for his promise to be fulfilled, he chose a young girl from Nazareth in Galilee. Her name was Mary. God filled her with his love and his grace and she kept her body and her soul free from every sin.

Mary was engaged to be married with Joseph, a good and just man, who was of the royal line of King David. God sent the Archangel Gabriel to announce to Mary that she would become **the mother of his son Jesus**. Mary was amazed at the news and wondered how this was possible. The angel explained to Mary: "the Holy Spirit will come down on you and the power of the most high God will cover you with its shadow. The child who will be born will be holy and will be called the Son of God!... Because nothing is impossible to God." (Lk 1:35,38)

Mary said yes straight away. She trusted in God completely and welcomed his plan for her. Joseph also welcomed God's will with faith.

The Son of God needed a mother and he needed someone who would be his father on earth, so that he would grow up in a family.

Jesus was born in Bethlehem, in the poverty of a stable. In heaven there was great joy! The angels went to give the announcement to some shepherds who were out in the hills that night with their sheep. They ran to adore him full of joy and amazement.

I bring you news of great joy. Today a saviour has been born to you!
Luke 2:10-12

He suffered under Pontius Pilate, was crucified, died and was buried

JESUS GAVE HIS LIFE OUT OF LOVE

Jesus went around Galilee healing the sick and forgiving sins, telling people about the love and mercy of God. When the time of the Passover feast arrived, Jesus went to Jerusalem together with his disciples. It was going to be the most important moment in human history, when salvation would finally arrive.

When they sat together at table to celebrate the feast, Jesus took the bread and broke it saying: "This is my body given for you." Then he took the wine and said: "This is my blood of the new covenant, given for you and for many for the forgiveness of sins". Jesus was telling his friends that he was about to give his life out of love.

That same night Jesus was arrested and taken before the high priest Caiaphas, the scribes and the elders. Then he was taken before Pontius Pilate the Roman governor.

Even though Jesus was innocent, he was condemned to death and handed over to the soldiers to be crucified.

On the cross, Jesus gave up his spirit to the father and asked God to forgive all those who were killing him. **He offered his life for the salvation of all human beings.**

His body was taken from the cross, wrapped in a sheet and placed in a tomb carved in the rock.

Then the entrance was closed with a heavy boulder.

> A man can have no greater love than to lay down his life for his friends.
> **John 15:13**

Jesus descended into hell, on the third day he rose again from the dead

JESUS IS THE LORD OF LIFE

Jesus wanted to share in all our experiences, even the ones that make us suffer and especially the worst of them all… death. But death had no power over Jesus because he is the Lord of Life!

Jesus went down to where all the people who had died before him, were waiting. The Jews call this place 'sheol'. In the Creed we call it hell. Jesus gave the good news to all the holy souls who were there waiting for the joy of the resurrection. He told them that heaven was now open!

In the meantime the apostles were confused, afraid and sad because their master was dead. They were all gathered together wondering what to do next.

At dawn on the third day after Jesus' death, some women who were disciples of Jesus went to the tomb to anoint their master's body with oils and perfumes.

When they arrived they found that the boulder had been moved and the tomb was empty. Something incredible had happened!

Then suddenly they saw an angel dressed in bright white clothing who said to them: "Do not be afraid! I know that you are looking for Jesus. He is not here, he is Risen!" (Mk 16:6)

They rushed back to tell the Apostles, but Peter and John wanted to see for themselves. So they ran to the tomb and saw that it was true: Jesus really was the Son of God and everything that he said would happen had come to pass.

The Resurrection of Jesus was the most important part of the good news that the disciples spread to the whole world.

Why look among the dead for someone who is alive? He is not here; he has risen.
Luke 24:5-6

Jesus ascended into heaven, and is seated at the right hand of God the Father Almighty

JESUS IN THE GLORY OF THE FATHER

After the resurrection, Jesus appeared many times to his disciples, but they didn't recognise him immediately because he was now full of glory and light.

Jesus sent them to bring the good news to the whole world; of God's infinite love for every creature, and that life was victorious over death. Jesus made a promise to his disciples that is still valid today. "I will be with you always, even to the end of time." (Mt 28:20)

Jesus blessed his disciples, then a cloud came down and covered him and they saw him go up into heaven.

Now Jesus sits at the right hand of God the Father: this means that Jesus is clothed with the power, honour and majesty of God.

St Paul asked all Christians to behave differently from the people around them who did not know Jesus. They should look to the things of heaven rather than those of Earth, and to think of the glorious risen Lord at all times so that they could be new creatures with him.

From his throne of light and of mercy, Jesus intercedes for us before God. He wants us to remain one body with him in the Church.

We believe what St Augustine said many centuries ago: "that Jesus is in heaven yet he is still with us. We live down here, yet we are already with him." Jesus is waiting for us and wants to open the doors of his Father's heavenly house for us. He wants us to be with him forever in his everlasting kingdom of love.

Since you have been brought back to true life with Christ, you must look for the things that are in heaven, where Christ is, sitting at God's right hand.
Colossians 3:1

He will come to judge the living and the dead

JESUS KNOWS OUR HEARTS

The Church and all its members are waiting for the second coming of Jesus, which will take place at the end of time. Like a just and merciful king, the Lord will come again in glory to defeat evil once and for all and to judge all human beings. But how will we be judged? Jesus told a parable to explain how it will be: his Kingdom is like a field where wheat and weeds grow together. When harvest time arrives, the farmer tells the reapers to collect the weeds in bundles and to burn them, but the wheat will be safely stored in the barn.

Jesus has shown us the path we should follow, but he has left us free to choose. This parable teaches us that we must decide for ourselves, moment by moment, what we wish to be and what our lives mean. We have to decide whether we want to be golden wheat, or weeds that only harm those around us.

Jesus will come again to welcome into his kingdom all those who have loved others in this life and recognised Jesus in their brothers and sisters, especially the smallest and least important.

Sitting on his throne of glory he will say: "I was hungry and you gave me food, I was thirsty and you gave me drink, I was a stranger and you welcomed me, naked and you clothed me, sick or in prison and you visited me… When you did this for the least of these brothers of mine, you did it for me!" (Mt 25:35-36,40)

In his words and in his example, Jesus told us that we would be judged on whether we have loved.

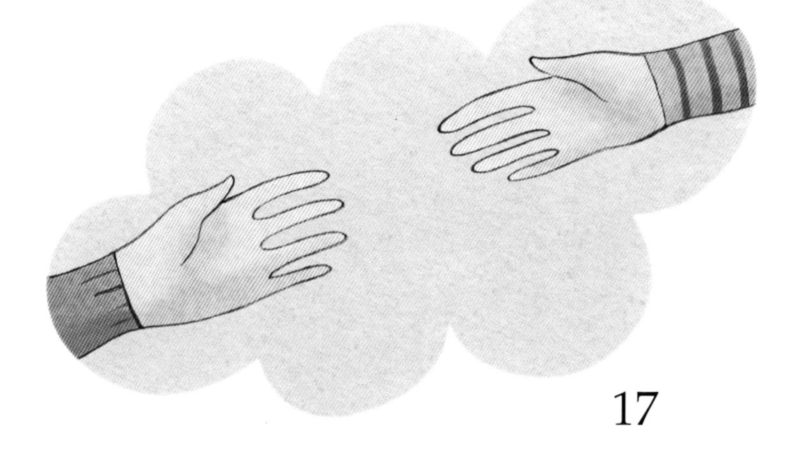

I believe in the Holy Spirit

THE POWERFUL BREATH OF GOD

The Holy Spirit is the third person of the Holy Trinity, deeply united to God the Father and the Son, Jesus.

On the day of Pentecost while the Twelve Apostles were gathered together with Mary, they suddenly heard a loud noise coming from heaven like a powerful wind. Tongues of fire appeared and came to rest on each of them, and **they were filled with the Holy Spirit.**

The Holy Spirit is like a great flame of fire, he is alive and powerful!

Like fire, the Holy Spirit gives light and energy and can change everything he touches.

In the Hebrew language the spirit is called 'ruah' which means wind, to blow, or breath... The wind that blew gently over the waters when the world was created, was the same powerful wind of the day of Pentecost, a wind which blows wherever it wants!

Often the Holy Spirit is represented as a dove, which is a sign of meekness and peace. A dove appeared over Jesus on the day of his baptism in the River Jordan. It is the Holy Spirit who helps us to know Jesus and reveals to us that he really is the Son of God.

We receive the Holy Spirit in a special way in the Sacrament of Confirmation. The Bishop anoints our forehead with the holy oil of Chrism, a sign of strength and the presence of the Holy Spirit at work in us.

The Spirit brings love, joy, peace, patience, kindness, goodness, trustfulness, gentleness and self-control

Galatians 5:22

I believe in the holy catholic Church, the communion of saints

THE PEOPLE OF GOD JOURNEYING TOWARDS HEAVEN

The Church is the people of God, called from every corner of the world to live in his presence. The word 'Church' comes from the Greek word 'ekklesia' which means 'assembly'. The word 'catholic' means 'universal' because the Church includes all the peoples of the earth.

The first who were called by Jesus were the Twelve Apostles, whom he chose to live side by side with him. They were simple men. Some were fishermen like Simon Peter and Andrew, James and John. Jesus said to them: "follow me and I will make you Fishers of men!" (Mt 4:19)

Once they had received the gift of the Holy Spirit, they began to spread the good news to everyone they met. The number of disciples grew from day to day. The first Christians began to live as a community, listening to the teachings of the Apostles. They took care of each other and lived as brothers and sisters, praising God together in the temple every day and meeting in each other's houses to celebrate the Eucharist.

The Church still meets together today to listen to the Word of God, to celebrate the Sacraments and to live in brotherly love.

The Church to which we belong is like a flock of sheep and Jesus is our shepherd. He loves his sheep and knows us all by name!

The Church is like a vine where grapes grow. Jesus is the true vine and we are the branches, we can only bear fruit if we are joined to him.

The church grew, living in the fear of the Lord, and filled with the consolation of the Holy Spirit.

Acts 9:31

I believe in the forgiveness of sins

GOD LOVES US AND FORGIVES US

God is a merciful Father who loves us with an infinite love. He trusts us and gives us freedom to think and act. He wants us to be happy and free from the chains of selfishness and evil.

In the Sacrament of Baptism he opens the doors of his house to us and we become his children, and the brothers and sisters of Jesus. We receive forgiveness for original sin and for all the sins we have committed too.

God knows our weaknesses and turns towards us every time we want to go back to him. To make this possible, he has entrusted the Church with the Sacrament of Reconciliation. In Confession, God forgives our sins and renews his friendship with us once more.

In a similar way, Jesus asks us to love and forgive our brothers and sisters and not to close our hearts - even to those who do evil to us! If we are at peace with others and have made up with them after an argument or a misunderstanding, then God welcomes and listens to our prayer and praise even more!

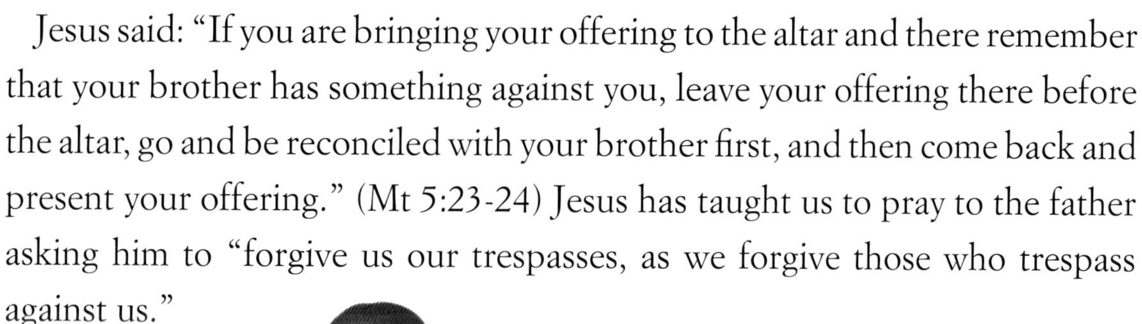

Jesus said: "If you are bringing your offering to the altar and there remember that your brother has something against you, leave your offering there before the altar, go and be reconciled with your brother first, and then come back and present your offering." (Mt 5:23-24) Jesus has taught us to pray to the father asking him to "forgive us our trespasses, as we forgive those who trespass against us."

I believe in the resurrection of the body

LIVING IN THE PRESENCE OF GOD IN BODY AND SOUL

In the book of Genesis we read that God the Father of Life made us in his own image and likeness and in his own marvellous plan. **He created us for life in both body and soul.**

God wanted his most beautiful creatures be happy and to live forever, but death entered into human history when Adam and Eve turned away from him and believed in the lies of the serpent.

In the eyes of God our body has a great dignity, it is the temple of our soul and our whole person is the temple of the Holy Spirit.

When he sent his Son into the world,
God wanted him to be a true man,
to share in the life that every human being lives.
God wanted Jesus to be formed in his mother's womb,
and to grow up like every other child.

Jesus is the new man, the new Adam! With his death and resurrection he defeated the power that death has over everyone. He appeared to his disciples with a glorious body to show them that he was not a ghost, but that he was truly risen. He said: "Look at my hands and my feet: it is I indeed!" (Lk 24:39) then he asked them for something to eat! We believe in the risen Jesus and we believe that we will rise from the dead as well, with the body that God created for us. Then our body too will enjoy the glory of God in heaven forever.

Then the risen Lord spoke to Thomas,
'Put your finger here; look,
here are my hands and my side.
Doubt no longer but believe.'
Luke 6:36-37

I believe in life everlasting

LIVING FOREVER IN GOD'S LOVE

On Earth we are pilgrims on a unique journey which will never be repeated. This journey does not end when we die because **Jesus promised us eternal life** to be with him forever. Our life is a journey towards our true home in the Father's house!

Jesus wants us to give the right importance to the things of this world, and not to worry too much about what we are to eat, drink or wear, because God the Father knows what we need: "Store up treasure for yourselves in heaven, where neither moth nor woodworms destroy them and thieves cannot break in and steal. For where your treasure is there will your heart be also." (Mt 6:20-21)

Jesus told a parable to explain what heaven will be like: It is like a wedding banquet which a King has prepared for his son. We are all invited to the party and we should go to meet our King dressed in beautiful clothes. These clothes are our soul, and it should be clean and shining, without creases or stains.

God has prepared a wonderful life for his friends in heaven. We will share this life with all the Saints who have ever lived, with Mary our Mother and with all the angels. This is the true and everlasting life God wants for us. Heaven is an everlasting happiness where the peace, joy and love for which God us will never end!

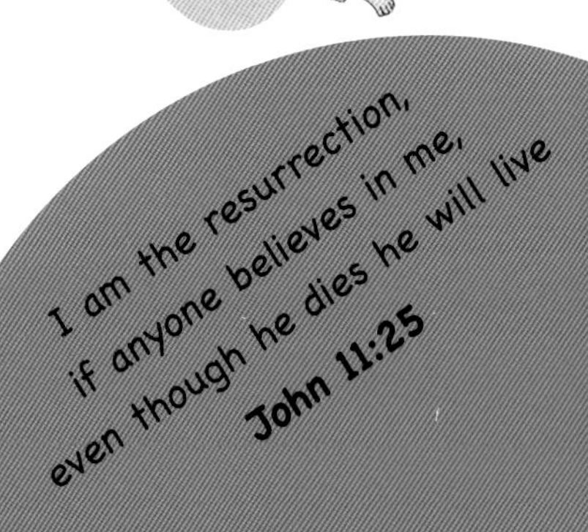

LET'S PLAY

EVERYTHING HAS ITS PLACE

Colour in the picture below and draw a line to connect each created thing with where it should live.

FIND THE SENTENCE

Put the letters below in the right order and discover the tenderness that God has for you.

Below, write the sentence you have found.

Colour in the pictures below from the life of Jesus.

TWO HIDDEN SYMBOLS

Colour in the shapes marked with a dot and discover one of the symbols of the Church.

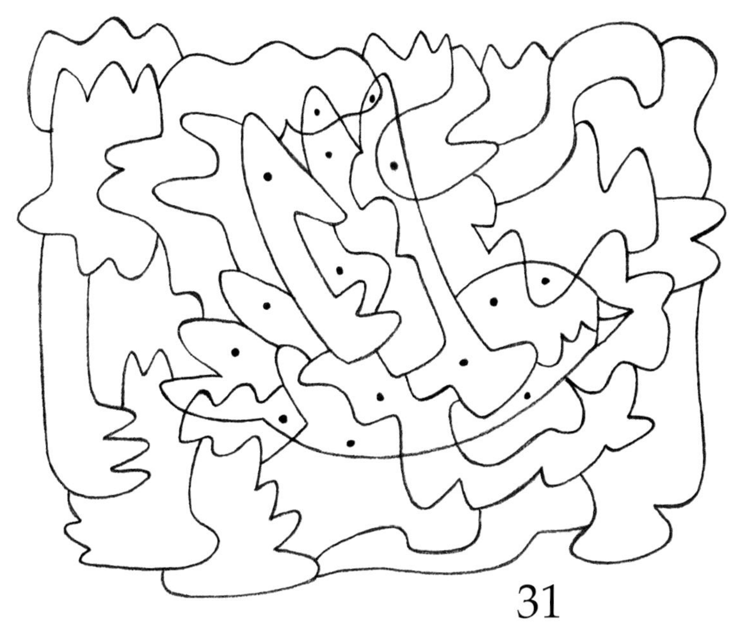

Colour in the shapes marked with a dot and discover one of the symbols of the Holy Spirit.

The Creed Explained for Children: Published 2013 by The Incorporated Catholic Truth Society, 40-46 Harleyford Road, London SE11 5AY. Tel: 020 7640 0042; Fax: 020 7640 0046; www.cts-online.org.uk.

ISBN: 978 1 86082 849 2 CTS Code CH 47

Translated from the original Italian Edition **Il Credo Spiegato ai Bambini** - ISBN 978-88-6124-228-9, published by Il Pozzo di Giacobbe, Gruppo Editoriale S.R.L., Cortile San Teodoro, 3, 91100 Trapani (TP), Italy